Sea Turtles

Focus: Endangered Animals

Meredith Costain

Sea turtles live in the sea. There are many kinds of sea turtles.

Sea turtles are at risk because people do not take care of them.

Sea turtles lay their eggs
on sandy beaches.
They lay their eggs
in a hole in the sand.

Sometimes people or animals
dig up their eggs for food.

Some people drop
plastic bags into the water.
The bags look like jellyfish.
If sea turtles eat the bags,
they die.

Fishers use big nets.
If sea turtles get trapped
in fishing nets, they drown.

People need to take care
of sea turtles.
There are not many sea
turtles left in the world.